THIS BOOK

365 DAILY MOTIVATIONAL QUOTES

to uplift, empower and inspire.

A daily guide to keep you focused on success in all aspects of life.

A. Douglas Webber

I LOVE THIS BOOK

CONTENTS:

* Introduction
* How to use this book
* Daily Quotes
* About the Author

*This book is dedicated in loving memory of **Lloyd Webber.** "cousin Lloyd ". God got an early angel.*

INTRODUCTION:

This book was written as a concise collection of quotes to help stimulate the mind and soul to find inspiration in every word. I've put together 365 of my favorite thoughts, ideas, quotes, contemplations, memes, reflections etc., to help motivate the readers thought process towards success. Some you've heard before, but probably not most. I purposely chose newer, unique, more modern phrases to inspire and challenge your intellectual spirit. Each quote builds upon the one the day before to increase the momentum of daily success thinking. This book of daily contemplations can be read year after year to further drive their meaning deeper into your subconscious behavior. It may only take one unheard of quote/idea to completely change your life and put you on the path you were destined to be on.

HOW TO USE THIS BOOK:

I love this book is a daily hand held pick me up. It's like your morning cup of coffee, but this mental jolt stays with you all day long. Every day, you are meant to read the quote for that day and memorize it, so it sticks. Try to think of the meaning on your own which will help stimulate your understanding of the thoughts. Try to contemplate the quotes as you use them in your daily life. Some quotes do have brief explanations, but most are meant for your own interpretation.

When I first started writing this book, I made a picture of each quote and made it my phone's screen saver for the day. It's been said that the average person checks their phone around 96 times a day. If you read the day's quote 96 times, it's almost impossible not to remember it. To take the time to go through the process of making it a screen saver makes you spend added time reading it until it's on your phone. That truly helps it to sink in. Certainly, you can write them down, which is also a great idea. Handwriting is associated with strong neural encoding, memory retrieval and more robust brain activity. *"handwriting to me, is simply thinking through my fingers"* …. Issac Asimov. So, whether you memorize it, write it down or make it into a screen saver, I hope you find some you can use, cherish, and maybe inspire you to write your own one day. Enjoy !

January 1st

80% of all decisions should be made when they first come up.

January 2nd

Winners focus on the results; losers focus on the activity.

January 3rd

Practice makes progress. **Jim Kwik**.

January 4th

It is impossible to fail if you succeed enough times.

January 5th

Ease is a greater threat to progress than hardship.

January 6th

I am not what happened to me, I am what I choose to become. **Carl Jung**

January 7th

A coward dies many times before their death; the valiant never taste of death but once. They experience fear and move forward.

January 8th

What advice would you give to the younger version of yourself.

January 9th

Life isn't about finding yourself, life is about creating yourself. **George Bernard Shaw.**

January 10th

Put yourself in a position where you cannot retreat. *Burn the boats.*

January 11th

We've been given the dignity of choice to become part of what we could be or all that we could be. **Zig Ziglar**

January 12th

Only those who risk going too far, can find out how far they can go.

January 13th

New levels bring new devils: You have to be tough. **T.D. Jakes**.

January 14th

When you change the input, the output changes automatically: change bad habits, routines, procrastination etc.

January 15th

You have to have a dream, if you want a dream to come true. **Brian Tracy**

January 16th

Before you do anything, ask yourself, what is the best use of my time, right now.

January 17th

Self-esteem is the foundation of all successful relationships.

January 18th

The fear of failure can be ended by having courage.

January 19th

Develop the quality of being unstoppable: nothing can stop me, and I'll never quit.

January 20th

Go confidently in the direction of your dreams and act as if it were impossible to fail. **Dorothy Brand**

January 21st

To get something you've never had, you have to do something you never did.

January 22nd

People do not buy products; they buy feelings and identities. Do more for your clients than anyone else; add more value.

January 23rd

Are you a meaning specific or a wandering generality? What is your life's work? **Jim Rohn**

January 24th

Let the universe know what you want, work hard towards it, and let go of how it comes to pass.

January 25th

Time is more valuable than money. You can get more money, but you can't get more time.

January 26th

When you hold onto your history, you do it at the expense of your destiny. **T. D. Jakes**

January 27th

Don't let your dreams, be dreams……………………

January 28th

You control where awareness goes and your energy flows.

January 29th

If you're tired of starting over, stop giving up.

January 30th

Have the courage to follow your heart and intuition, they somehow already know what you truly want to become.
Steve Jobs

January 31st

Find out what you want and go for like your life depends on it: why, because it does.

February 1st

You have to acknowledge that what you're chasing means more than what you're leaving behind.

February 2nd

It's better to be hated for what you are than to be loved for what you're not.

February 3rd

Do the thing you fear, and the death of fear is certain. **Mark Twain**

February 4th

When you believe it, you will see it.

February 5th

Everything you do for yourself, you take with you. Everything you do for others, you leave behind. **Less Brown**.

February 6th

Our life is our gift from God: how we live our life is our gift to God. **Less Brown.**

February 7th

If you want to succeed as much as you want to breathe, then you will be successful. **Eric Taylor**

February 8th

Don't cry about the pain, cry about the joy of success. **Eric Taylor.**

February 9th

You should be able at any moment to sacrifice what you are, for what you will become.

February 10th

At the end of pain is success.

February 11th

The effect you have on others is the most valuable currency there is. **Jim Carrey**

February 12th

There's no gain without pain.

February 13th

Your philosophy determines what you do with all the obstacles and opportunities you face. **Jim Rohn**.

February 14th

Dreams are free, but the journey isn't.

February 15th

Ideation without execution is delusion.

February 16th

Courage is the ability to do things that are uncertain.

February 17th

We can't get anything in our life that we're not first wired for. You can't get wealthy unless you're wired for wealth. *(Reprogram your subconscious mind)* **Dr. Joe Dispenza**

February 18th

Discipline keeps you from giving into your desires and short-term gratification.

February 19th

Dare to go forward in the direction of fulfilling your potential.

February 20th

There's no security in life, only opportunity: the more we seek opportunity, the more security we have. **General MacArthur**

February 21st

Nothing succeeds like success.

February 22nd

Treat your energy as if it were money: protect it, invest it wisely and manage it well.

February 23rd

Never compromise your peace of mind.

February 24th

Your potential expands as you move towards it. **Marisa Peer.**

February 25th

If you don't like who you are, you have to change what you **think** you should be.

February 26th

You only work 8 hours a day for survival; everything over 8 hours is for success.

February 27th

Action without thinking is the cause of every failure.

February 28th

Knowing you are going to die is the best way to avoid the trap of thinking you have something to lose. **Steve Jobs**

March 1st

Intuition will always give you the right answer.

March 2nd

Mentally rehearse the Who you'd like to be. **A. Douglas Webber**

March 3rd

If you don't know where you're going, any road will take you there.

March 4th

To be successful, do what's hard and necessary and not what's fun and easy.

March 5th

You can't be scared to fail; failure is the next step to success.

March 6th

If you're in a job you don't love, get out of it like it's a burning house.

March 7th

If you don't pay the price for success, you'll pay the price for failure. **Zig Ziglar**

March 8th

What you resist, persists. **Carl Jung**. Focus *__only__* on what you want in life.

March 9th

To end *procrastination*: when you start to procrastinate, say, "DO It Now, Do It Now, Do It Now", and then do whatever it is.

March 10th

The more you do of what you're doing, the more you'll get of what you've got.

March 11th

Greatness cannot be achieved without obsession.

March 12th

If you don't do it, nothing is possible. If you do it, everything is possible.

March 13th

I'll tell you how risky life is: "you're not going to get out alive. **Zig Ziglar**

March 14th

Money comes to me easily and frequently. (Daily mantra)

March 15th

You become what you think about all day long.

March 16th

Nothing can stop you, if don't stop for anything. **Eric Thomas**.

March 17th

The only thing you need right now is, whatever it takes.

March 18th

What does the world need that your talent can provide? **Jim Carrey**

March 19th

If you do what is easy, your life will be hard. If you do what is hard, your life will be easy.

March 20th

You have to feel gratitude every day in order for your new experience to occur. **Dr. Joe Dispenza**

March 21st

If you want to produce great acorns, think like an Oak tree, not like an acorn.

March 22nd

Work to your potential, not to your quota.

March 23rd

It's not the hours you put in, it's what you put in the hours. **Jim Rohn**

March 24th

The purpose of life is a life of purpose.

March 25th

Easy choices; hard life. Hard choices, easy life. (The hard choices; what we most fear doing, asking, saying; these are often exactly what we most often need to do)

March 26th

We are so afraid of the future, when the only thing that should scare us, is repeating the past.

March 27th

Human beings absolutely follow through on who they believe they are. **Tony Robbins.**

March 28th

If you are what you didn't want to be, it's because of the dreams or goals you forgot to set in the past.

March 29th

Only 3 % of adults have written goals: everyone else works for them.

March 30th

In your job/career: what would you love to do 7 days a week: do that.

March 31st

My life is my message. **Ghandi**

April 1st

Know how you are smart, not how smart you are.

April 2nd

Ask yourself everyday: *"how would the person I'd like to be, do the things I'm about to do"?*

April 3rd

Commit yourself to becoming excellent.

April 4th

Everything that irritates us about others can lead us to an understanding about ourselves. **Carl Jung**

April 5th

Take your awareness and focus on what you want; that's where your energy flows, when your energy flows there, it starts to manifest in your life.

April 6th

Make self-belief so normal, that everyone else believes in you too. **Marisa Peer**

April 7th

What goals would you set if you knew it was impossible to fail.

April 8th

The tendency to seek security is the low road to failure. **Hellen Keller**

April 9th

<u>Without obstacles, no success is possible</u>.

April 10th

Discipline hurts for a little while, but regret is long term.

April 11th

Your attitude is your prophet of your future. Your attitude determines your happiness and success in life more than anything else.

April 12th

Look yourself in the mirror and ask yourself: *"what do I want to do every day for the rest of my life "*and do it.
Gary Vaynerchuk

April 13th

You are what you thought you should be.

April 14th

The very successful person allocates and thinks of time in minutes, not hours, days, morning, noon, and night.

April 15th

Is how I'm spending my time, in alignment with my major goals?

April 16th

Salami slice big projects. Take a task and break it up into small pieces.

April 17th

We all act consistent with who we believe we are. **Tony Robbins**

April 18th

What's my job: what results are expected of me: why am I on the payroll?

April 19th

Make rock bottom the foundation on which to rebuild your life.

April 20th

He who has a WHY to live, can bear almost any HOW. **Nietzsche**

April 21st

Raise your standards. Change your shoulds to musts. **Tony Robbins**

April 22nd

If you put a frog in boiling water, he'll jump right out. But, if you put it in and slowly turn up the heat, he'll die. *Change your environment*.

April 23rd

If you are ordering easy, I hope you enjoy the dessert: it's the disgusting taste of regret.

April 24th

Live your life to the fullest, so your eulogy becomes the greatest story ever told. **A. Douglas Webber**

April 25th

Be relentless in the pursuit of your goals, especially in the face of obstacles. Along the way, make no excuses and place no blame. **Ray Bourque**

April 26th

In any given moment we have two options: to step forward in growth, or step back into safety. **Abraham Maslow**

April 27th

Between stimulus and response there is a space. In that space is the power to choose our response. In our responses lies our growth and our freedom.

April 28th

When you talk, you are repeating what you already know. But if you listen, you may learn something new.
Dalai Lama

April 29th

Don't pursue happiness, pursue a lifestyle that results in happiness.
Dandapani

April 30th

95 % of everything you do is a result of habit.

May 1st

To earn more, you must learn more; one hour a day on personal growth.

May 2nd

The privilege of a lifetime is to become who you truly are. **Carl Jung**

May 3rd

Treat your energy the same way you treat money – manage-allocate-invest. **Dandapani.**

May 4th

If you're not early, you're late.

May 5th

Only a person who risks is free.

May 6th

Preoccupation with a good thing is no substitute for the right thing.

May 7th

If someone had to think of something that reminded them of you, what would it be?

May 8th

You can fail at what you don't want, so you might as well take a chance at doing what you love. **Jim Carrey**

May 9th

Decide, Commit, Act, Succeed, Repeat.

May 10th

The billionaire and the beggar both have 24 hours a day.

May 11th

You cannot stop a day, you cannot stop an hour, but you can control how it will be used. **Dr. Myles Monroe**.

May 12th

Your path is made by walking it.

May 13th

Do what you love: you cannot be successful if you're not doing what you love.

May 14th

Life is a manifestation of where you direct your energy. **Dandapani**

May 15th

Practice concentration, not distraction: focus every day on **who** and **what** is important.

May 16th

Things don't happen to me, they happen for me. They only happen for me when I'm making progress towards something.

May 17th

Life is a gift, so live it in the present. **A. Douglas. Webber**

May 18th

No one can live beyond the limits of their beliefs. If you want to live beyond what you're living now, you have to change your beliefs.

May 19th

Your life is what you think it should be.

May 20th

For a committed person, there's no such thing as failure. If you fall down 100 times, there's 100 lessons learned. **Sadhguru**

May 21st

The outcome is not the thing that needs to change, it's the systems that precede it.

May 22nd

Sight is the ability to see things as they are. Vision is the capacity to see things as they can be. **Dr. Myles Monroe**

May 23rd

The word problem is a human definition for an opportunity to grow. Think of the word problem as a positive.

May 24th

Known hells are preferable to strange heavens: Don't stay in a bad situation…….

May 25th

Do not go where the path may lead, but go where there's no path, and leave a trail. **Henry Theroux**

May 26th

You must make fear and failure your best friend in order to move the needle towards life.

May 27th

Greatness cannot be achieved without obsession.

May 28th

Be the most important person to the world.

May 29th

What follows "I **AM** ", will always come looking for you: I am creative, I am lucky, I am smart……………

May 30th

Paying bills will push you to earn a living, but becoming wealthy will pull you towards that goal: What is your why?

May 31st

If you live each day as if it were your last, someday you'll most certainly be right.

June 1st

The angels who will guide you throughout your life, will only be there for you when they recognize themselves in you. **Wayne Dyer.**

June 2nd

Look yourself in the mirror every day and ask, "if today were your last day of my life, would I want to do what I'm about to do today". Whenever the answer is no for too many days in a row, you need to change something. **Steve Jobs.**

June 3rd

You can't make a difference until you make a decision.

June 4th

Are you going through it, or growing through it?

June 5th

Your passion should wake you up, not your alarm clock.

June 6th

Invest your energy and time into people and things as if it was your money: ……invest your time like you would your money. **Dandapani**.

June 7th

Only those who can see the invisible can do the impossible.

June 8th

In life we must all suffer one of two pains: the pain of discipline or the pain of regret.

June 9th

If you died at this moment, what would die with you?

June 10th

Your philosophy is the major determining factor in how your life turns out. **Jim Rohn**

June 11th

The people who are crazy enough to think they can change then world, are the ones who do.

June 12th

When you are not pursuing your goals, you are committing spiritual suicide.

June 13th

Reprogram your **sub-conscious mind** through affirmations; precise words, visualize and with emotions.

June 14th

To show compassion, see life through the lens of love. **A. Douglas Webber**

June 15th

Adversity introduces a person to themselves.

June 16th

Time is the only commodity on earth, given equally to every human being.

June 17th

Whenever there is a argument between your heart and mind, follow your heart.

June 18th

Take your dreams and breathe your own personal spirit into it, until it becomes a flame that burns around the world. **Jim Rohn**.

June 19th

For your career: What is it that you could do seven days a week, that'll bring a smile to your face ? **Les Brown**

June 20th

You cannot have an attitude beyond your belief. **Dr. Myles Munroe**.

June 21st

I prefer brutal honesty over hypocritical politeness.

June 22nd

Have the faith of a child's dream: ***dream-believe-achieve-repeat***.

June 23rd

Find something that separates you from everyone else on earth, and until you do, you will be stressed and struggling. **Tony Robbins**

June 24th

The higher you raise your *self-image*, the fewer judgements and manipulations you will tolerate.

June 25th

Confidence is the willingness to try. **Mel Robbins**

June 26th

Having the talent to succeed doesn't compare to having the guts to fail. **A. Douglas Webber**

June 27th

The effort of making the attempt is progress. **Ray Lewis**

June 28th

There're people in the hospital, begging God for the *opportunity* you have right now. **T. D. Jakes**.

June 29th

You are a perfect reflection of the hard work or lack of work you put in.

June 30th

There's good news and bad news. The bad news is, Time Flies. The good news is, you are the pilot. **Jay Shetty**

July 1st

FEAR: **F**alse **E**vidence **A**ppearing **R**eal.

July 2nd

What you get by achieving your goal is not as important as what you become by achieving your goals. **Jim Rohn**.

July 3rd

When people take the courage to journey into the center of their Fear, they find nothing. It's only many layers of fear being afraid of itself.

July 4th

Work hard, until one day your signature becomes an autograph.

July 5th

People operate within the context of the vision they have for themselves.

July 6th

What people think about you and the possibility of your dreams, is none of your business. **Les Brown**

July 7th

Success is the artistic interpretation of your own imagination.

July 8th

You Can't Fly Without Gravity................................ **Jim Rohn**

July 9th

Be a thermostat, not a thermometer. **Jim Kwik**

July 10th

Life is too short to play the wrong sport. **A. Douglas Webber**

July 11th

Obstacles are what you see when you lose sight of your goals.

July 12th

You only get one shot at life, make it memorable.

July 13th

Your destiny is the consequence of your daily decisions.

July 14th

Follow your bliss, and the universe will open doors where there were only walls. **Joseph Campbell**

July 15th

When you were born, you cried while the world rejoiced. Live your life in such a way, that when you die, the world cries, while you rejoice.

July 16th

Ask yourself what impact this goal will have on my future.

July 17th

A gift is the inherent capacity to fulfill a function that meets a need in creation. **Dr. Myles Monroe**

July 18th

One person with a belief overrides a thousand people with only intent.

July 19th

Life's not about where you start or where you end; it's about the distance you travel. What kind of legacy will you leave?

July 20th

Live life, as if everything is rigged in your favor. **Rumi**

July 21st

How you make your money is more important than how much money you make. **Gary V**.

July 22nd

It's never too late to be what you might have been. **George Eliot**.

July 23rd

You have to take advantage of an opportunity of a lifetime, in the lifetime of the opportunity.

July 24th

What is it that you do at your absolute best, with the least amount of effort. That's your gift. **Steve Harvey**

July 25th

Impossible is not a fact, it's an opinion.

July 26th

You have to feel abundant for your wealth to find you. **Dr. Joe Dispenza**

July 27th

Used to be's don't make no honey: the past is the past, who are you now……

July 28

Success is in the journey, not the reaching of the goal.

July 29th

If no one thinks you're crazy, you're not yet operating to the outer limits of your potential. **Brandon Burchard**

July 30th

Believe it is already yours; close your eyes and see your dreams.

July 31st

In any given moment, we have two options; to step forward into growth, or to step back into safety. **Abraham Maslow**

August 1st

You have to embed in your subconscious, that you were meant to be successful.

August 2nd

Ambition is the path to success, persistence is the vehicle you arrive in. **Bill Bradley**

August 3rd

It's fine to celebrate success, but it's more important to heed the lessons of failure. **Bill Gates**

August 4th

The strongest force in the entire human personality is the need to stay consistent with how we define ourselves. **Tony Robbins**.

August 5th

There's no such thing as failure, only feedback.

August 6th

If you're tired of starting over, stop giving up.

August 7th

The only person you have to be better than is the person you were yesterday.

August 8th

Rest in the assumption that you already are who you want to be. **Dr. Wayne Dyer**

August 9th

Energy flows where attention goes.

August 10th

Crisis comes to serve the person who wants to use it as fuel.

August 11th

You have to acknowledge that what you are chasing means more to you than what you are leaving behind.

August 12th

Faith is the ability to see things that don't exist yet. **Jim Rohn**.

August 13th

The best thing you can do to make a difference is to first become a better person yourself.

August 14th

Decide, commit, act, succeed, repeat.

August 15th

Vanity and arrogance equal Fear.

August 16th

Hard work beats talent, if talent doesn't work hard.

August 17th

Your attitude is the paintbrush of the mind. **John Maxwell**

August 18th

Being conventional makes no room for creativity. Change your environment, friends, attitude etc. **Dr. Myles Munroe**

August 19th

Your gift is the thing you do your absolute best, with the least amount of effort. **Steve Harvey**

August 20th

Life is a manifestation of where your energy is flowing (where you direct your energy) **Dandapani**.

August 21st

What will make you truly, truly happy? Be exact and specific. How will you know when you've got it?

August 22nd

The most intense fight a person will ever have is between the person they are, and the person they are capable of becoming.

August 23rd

The words that follow **I am**, follow you.......What you say about you, will become you.

August 24th

Start every morning by saying: *"today wherever I go, I will create a peaceful, loving and joyful world"*. **Sadhguru**

August 25th

I have the courage to live the life that I know I'm destined to live.

August 26th

Doing a little bit every day is a lot more important than doing a lot someday.

August 27th

Faith is the oil that takes the friction out of living.

August 28th

Whether you think you can or can't, either way, you are right. Henry Ford.

August 29th

Think and act like the person you intend to become.

August 30th

The greatest failure of successful people is that of regret.

August 31st

Immerse yourself in the atmosphere that fuels your passion, until you become that atmosphere. **A. Douglas Webber**

September 1st

If you're happy, happy things will happen………….

September 2nd

Risk going for the life you want, or guarantee living the with one you don't want.

September 3rd

Leave the world a better place because you were here.

September 4th

Right now, you are the sum total of where you've been investing your energy, throughout your entire life. **Dandapani**

September 5th

The traits that make you strange are the gifts that make you special.

September 6th

Sweat more in training and bleed less in battle.

September 7th

If you're not defined by a vision of the future, you're left with the memories of the past. **Dr. Joe Dispenza**

September 8th

Worrying is praying for something you don't want.

September 9th

You make your beliefs, then your beliefs make you.

September 10th

Your mind is always ease dropping on your self-talk. Be careful what you say to yourself. **Jim Kwik**.

September 11th

We don't see things as they are, we see things as we are.

September 12th

Indecision is the thief of opportunity.

September 13th

Change happens when the pain of staying the same becomes greater than the pain of making a change.

September 14th

Tough times don't last, tough people do.

September 15th

The bridge between reality and a dream is work.

September 16th

MANTRA: I have the ability to build an unstoppable business that serves people all over the world.

September 17th

Your personality creates your personal reality. Personality: how you think, act, and feel. **Dr. Joe Dispenza**

September 18th

You attract what you are. **Wayne Dyer**

September 19th

The greatest risk you take is not taking one.

September 20th

Every set back is a set up for a comeback.

September 21st

Your purpose in life is the one thing you feel supremely qualified to tach other people.

September 22nd

Live full, die empty.

September 23rd

A question opens the mind; a statement closes the mind. Never say, I can't afford it; Ask, how can I afford it. Etc., etc.....

September 24th

It's always now; the reality of your life is now. Now is the new later. **Dr. Joe Dispenza.**

September 25th

Don't cry to give up. Cry to keep going. **Eric Thomas.**

September 26th

You can either be host to God, or a hostage to your ego. (Every moment of your life, this choice is yours) **Dr. Wayne Dyer.**

September 27th

Life is death, without change / without change, life is death. **Chris Angel**

September 28th

We all want to be with someone who makes us happy, when what we need to do is BE someone who makes us happy. **Jay Shetty**

September 29th

Failure is success in progress. **Einstein**

September 30th

The harder you work, the harder it is to surrender/give up. **Inky Johnson**

October 1st

First you make your beliefs, then your beliefs make you. **Marisa Peer**.

October 2nd

Use **failure** as **fuel** = *fuellure*. **A. Douglas Webber**

October 3rd

If you work hard on your job, you can make a living; if you work hard on yourself, you can make a fortune. **Jim Rohn**

October 4th

The only way you can is to know you can; you can't be, until you know.

October 5th

The ghost of your untried dreams, ideas, plans and goals will die along with you. They will cry with shame at your funeral.

October 6th

Only those who can see the invisible can do the impossible.

October 7th

In the land of the blind, the one-eyed man is king…………….

October 8th

You have to feel empowered in order for your success to show up. **Dr. Joe Dispenza.**

October 9th

If you point a finger forward, there are three pointing backward……. Make sure you're not the problem first.

October 10th

You always get more of what you're thankful for.

October 11th

Don't wait for your future to happen by chance; visualize and create your future in advance. **A. Douglas Webber** (change cause and effect to, causing an effect)

October 12th

Choose to be happy, instead of craving what you don't have.

October 13th

If you want to know what kind of life you've lived, start with your eulogy, and work your way backwards.

October 14th

Life doesn't give you what you want, it gives you what you deserve. **Eric Thomas**

October 15th

Face your fears: behind every fear is the person you'd like to be.

October 16th

If you do tomorrow what you did today, you'll get tomorrow what you got today.

October 17th

The bridge between reality and a dream is **work**.

October 18th

You can only control three things in your life: your thoughts, visions, and actions. Control these and you control your life. **Jack Canfield** (how you use those three things determines everything you experience)

October 19th

Strive every day to live up to God's expectation of you.

October 20th

All you see in the world is the outcome of your idea about it.

October 21st

The secret to getting ahead is getting started. **Mark Twain**.

October 22nd

Never let what you cannot do, interfere with what you can do. **John Wooton** (Do something now)

October 23rd

Every day for the rest of my life, I'm going to do whatever it takes to be the Angel in heaven God brags about. **A. Douglas Webber**

October 24th

You are not a product of your circumstances, but rather a product of your decisions. **Steven Covey**

October 25th

All behaviors are belief driven: Change your beliefs to change your behavior.

October 26th

Your imagination is the only thing that separates you from everyone else.

October 27th

Dare to go forward in the direction of your potential.

October 28th

Your purpose in life would be the one thing you feel supremely qualified to teach other people.

October 29th

Life is a mirror: Life gives us not what, life gives us who we are.

October 30th

Don't let the noise of other's opinions drown out your own inner voice. **Steve Jobs.**

October 31st

If you could live your life over again, would you. If yes, its never too late to change.

November 1st

You'll see it when you believe it. Live as is if your future dreams are a present fact. **Dr. Wayne Dyer**.

November 2nd

Hustle is the most important word ever. **Gary Vaynerchuk**

November 3rd

I am my own master and I avoid other people's opinions to affect me.

November 4th

Every morning and throughout the day say, "today, wherever I go, I will create a peaceful, loving and joyful world" **Sadhguru**

November 5th

Discipline is the bridge between goals and accomplishment.

November 6th

<u>"Wherever you go, there you are"</u>. Fix yourself first, if not, you'll keep showing up. You can't escape your old, bad habits by running from them.

November 7th

Pain is the currency of transformation.

November 8th

If Mother Teresa and Gandhi had a baby; live as if you were their child. **A. Douglas Webber**

November 9th

The secret to success is doing a lot of little things consistently, over a long period of time.

November 10th

The value of something is only equal to the sacrifice you made to get it.

November 11th

It's better to try and fail, then fail to try.

November 12th

If you just run after what's in front of you, you will escape what's behind you. **T. D. Jakes**

November 13th

The secret to getting ahead is getting started. The secret to getting started is breaking your complex, overwhelming tasks into small, manageable tasks, and then starting on the first one. **Mark Twain**

November 14th

When we forgive, we set a prisoner free, and discover that the prisoner we set free is us. **Lewis Smedes**

November 15th

Vision is the key to a successful life. God did not create you to have life happen to you. You were designed to happen to life.

November 16th

Nothing has more value than your sense of inner peace. Practice saying, "***I'll handle it***".

November 17th

If you want to be **happy**, set a goal that commands your thoughts, liberates your energy, and inspires your hopes. **Andrew Carnegie.**

November 18th

You want to set a goal that is big enough, that in the process of achieving it, you become someone worth becoming. **Jim Rohn**.

November 19th

When life gets tough, get tougher.

November 20th

Program the script in your mind, until you become the script.

November 21st

Strive for perfection, settle for excellence.

November 22nd

85% of people let their fear of failure outweigh their desire to succeed.

November 23rd

Without commitment, you'll never start and without consistency, you'll never finish. **Denzel Washington**.

November 24th

Leap afraid, and then gather your courage on the way down. **Lisa Nichols**

November 25th

Don't let your tombstone be the only mark you left behind. **A Douglas Webber**

November 26th

To become who you might be, you have to walk away from what you are.

November 27th

Yesterday is history, tomorrow is a mystery, **today** is a gift, that's why it's called the present.

November 28th

Only see yourself as the way you wish to be.

November 29th

Goals must be very specific, clear, and written.

November 30th

We think in pictures; If you can't see your future, you'll never get there.

December 1st

The greatest hazard in life is to risk nothing. **Less Brown**.

December 2nd

Most people tip toe through life hoping they make it safely to death.

December 3rd

If you're not willing to pay the price, you don't deserve the reward.

December 4th

Have an attitude of **<u>GLADDITUDE</u>**. Be happy for what you have. **A. Douglas Webber**

December 5th

There's no such thing as a dumb question. *The dumb question is the one you didn't ask.*

December 6th

Sometimes by losing the battle, you find a new way to win the war.

December 7th

Logic will get you from A to B: Imagination will take you everywhere. **Albert Einstein.**

December 8th

If you're still alive, you haven't reached your best yet.

December 9th

Your thoughts control your feelings, your feelings control your actions, and your actions control your events. When you take control of your thinking, it changes your life. **Merissa Peer**.

December 10th

Fear is the excuse your brain uses against you, when it's not convinced you deserve your goal. **A. Douglas Webber**

December 11th

Sacrificing short term pleasure for long term gain is the essential underlying theme to every person who's ever achieved meteoric success.

December 12th

All we are, is the result of what we've thought. **Buddha**

December 13th

Believe you can, and you're halfway there. **Teddy Roosevelt**

December 14th

Where are you supposed to be? Based on your dreams, based on your goals, based on your vision; where are you supposed to be? you can't stay the same and get to where you're supposed to be. **Walter Bond**

December 15th

Your words set the direction of your life, like a tiny rudder controls a large ship.

December 16th

Your plan for success has to be clear, concise, compelling, consistent, and committed.

December 17th

Dream as if you'll live forever, live as if you'll die today. **James Dean**

December 18th

Your vision will become clear only when you can look into your own heart. Who looks outside, dreams: who looks inside, awakes. **Carl Jung**

December 19th

If people are doubting how far you can go, go so far that you can't hear them.
Michele Ruiz

December 20th

Everything you can imagine is real.
Pablo Picasso

December 21st

Smart people learn from everything, and everyone, average people learn from their experiences, stupid people already have all the answers. **Socrates**

December 22nd

DAILY MANTRA: *Everything always goes right for me*………Say it all day long.

December 23rd

Feel the joy and happiness of what you want and expect.

December 24th

Problems are to the mind, what exercise is to the muscles: they toughen and make strong. **Norman Vincent Peale**

December 25th

PROBORTUNITY: look for the opportunity in every problem.

December 26th

When you stretch your mind to a new dimension, it never, ever, ever goes back, because your potential expands as you move towards it. **Marissa Peer**

December 27th

Proceed with confidence: believe in your ability to manifest something in your life.

December 28th

If you want to kill a big dream, tell it to a small minded person. **Steve Harvey**

December 29th

Someday is code for never.

December 30th

Go to bed early, wake up early, and when the opportunity clock goes off, don't hit the loose button. **A. Douglas Webber**

December 31st

Contemplate yourself as surrounded by the conditions which you wish to produce. **Dr. Wayne Dyer**.

NOTES:

ABOUT THE AUTHOR:

A. Douglas Webber, aka Tony, is a lifelong consumer of the best motivational and inspirational material available. Born and raised in Washington, DC, his thirst for that knowledge started as a teenager. His father was selling **Amway** products and started bringing home the suggested reading books, and Tony started reading them. The classics in those days were "**The richest man in Babylon**", **The magic of thinking big**", "**The greatest salesman in the world**" and "**The power of positive thinking**". Later on, after learning about the power of **paradigms**, he stumbled across another Tony, last name Robbins. Mr. Webber actually still listens to cassette tapes to this day from a 1992 **Tony Robbins** box set. He also listens to tapes from **Zig Ziglar**, **Brian Tracy**, **Napoleon Hill,** and **Jim Rohn**. Later in his **Pre-Paid Legal** days a new mountain of motivation erupted. Again, he immersed himself in CD's, DVD's, and books. The hit books at that time were, "**Who moved my cheese**", "**Don't sweat the small stuff**" and "**The question behind the question**". After devouring the **Law of Attraction** theory and going to several seminars by the top motivational speakers in the country, the author discovered the spiritual side of inspiration. Books like "**A course in miracles**", "**The power of intention**" by **Dr. Wayne Dyer** and **Power vs. Force**" by **Dr. David R. Hawkins**, changed his life. Those books, courses, DVD's, CD's, seminars etc. introduced Mr. Webber to an unending study of the world of the **ego**. That subject has been a major focus of his for the past 16 years. Currently, it's morning, noon and night in headphones listening and watching all the top speaker's greatest material on inspiration. That lifetime of constant study and dedication to this field of personal development, the ego and reprogramming the sub-conscious mind, is how he's been able to deliver this material here, so that one day you'll be able to say, "*I Love This Book*".

Made in the USA
Columbia, SC
28 July 2024